Stan the Stunt Snail

By Cath Jones

Illustrated by
Dean Gray

"I am good at stunts," Fliss boasted.

"I am a stunt star!"

"Yes!" Fliss said.

"You can be a stunt snail."

But Stella was not keen.

What if Stan fell?

"I am good at jumping!" Fliss boasted.

"Can you help me to do stunts?"

Stan said.

Fliss hopped onto a ladder.

"Hop on," she said.

Stan trusted Fliss, but Stella did not!

Stan hung on to the ladder.

At the top, Fliss did a handstand.

Oops!

"Stan, wait!" Stella said.

"You need the right kit."

She got Stan a stunt helmet

and pads for his shell.

"I am a stunt star," Fliss said.

She did a backflip off the ladder.

Fliss said, "JUMP!"

"Stan, wait!" Stella said.

"Fliss is NOT a stunt star!"

But Stan and Fliss got set to jump!

Stan shot down the ladder like a rocket.
But a big gust of wind lifted Fliss into
the air!

"Wow-ee. This is fun!" Stan said.

But Fliss fell!

"Help!" Fliss yelled.

Fliss and Stan landed in the web.

"Good job, Stella!" Fliss said.

"You are a stunt star!"

Quiz

1. What does Stan want to be?
a) A small snail
b) A stunt snail
c) A super snail

2. Who does Stan ask to help him to do stunts?
a) Fliss
b) Fran
c) Stella

3. Who does not trust Fliss?
a) Stan
b) Fran
c) Stella

4. What makes Fliss fall off the ladder?

a) A big gust of wind

b) Water on the ladder

c) A web

5. What does Stella spin to save Stan and Fliss?

a) A helmet

b) A web

c) A ladder

Turn over for answers

26/7/24.

Book Bands for Guided Reading

The Institute of Education book banding system is a scale of colours that reflects the various levels of reading difficulty. The bands are assigned by taking into account the content, the language style, the layout and phonics. Word, phrase and sentence level work is also taken into consideration.

Maverick Early Readers are a bright, attractive range of books covering the pink to white bands. All of these books have been book banded for guided reading to the industry standard and edited by a leading educational consultant.

To view the whole Maverick Readers scheme, visit our website at
www.maverickearlyreaders.com

Or scan the QR code above to view our scheme instantly

Quiz Answers: 1b, 2a, 3c, 4a, 5b